Nursery rhymes in this book

6   Twink'
     The m

8   Wee W
     Diddle

10   Hush-

11   Star light, star bright

12   Niddledy, noddledy
     Come, let's to bed

15   Where should a baby rest?
     How many miles to Babyland

16   The evening is coming

17   Now the day is over

18   Moon, sun, shiny and silver

19   I see the moon

20   The Sandman comes

21   Goodnight, sleep tight

22   Come to the window

23   Baby's boat's a silver moon

24   Sleepy-time has come for my baby
     Lullaby and goodnight

26   Rock-a-bye, baby
     Go to bed first

28   Sleep, little child
     Go to bed late

Published by Ladybird Books Ltd
A Penguin Company
Penguin Books Ltd., 80 Strand, London WC2R 0RL, UK
Penguin Books Australia Ltd., Ringwood, Victoria, Australia
Penguin Books (NZ) Ltd., Private Bag 102902, NSMC, Auckland, New Zealand
1 3 5 7 9 10 8 6 4 2
© LADYBIRD BOOKS LTD MMIV

Printed in Italy

Bedtime Rhymes

Illustrated by Lesley Harker

Ladybird

Twinkle, twinkle, little star

Twinkle, twinkle, little star,
How I wonder what you are!
Up above the world so high,
Like a diamond in the sky.
Twinkle, twinkle, little star,
How I wonder what you are!

The man in the moon

The man in the moon
Came tumbling down,
And asked the way to Norwich.

He went by south,
And burnt his mouth
With supping cold pease porridge.

7

Wee Willie Winkie

Wee Willie Winkie
Runs through the town,
Upstairs and downstairs
In his nightgown.
Rapping at the window,
Crying through the lock,
"Are the children all in bed,
For now it's eight o'clock!"

Diddle, diddle, dumpling

Diddle, diddle, dumpling,
My son John
Went to bed with his trousers on.
One shoe off, and one shoe on,
Diddle, diddle, dumpling,
My son John.

Hush-a-bye, baby

Hush-a-bye, baby, on the treetop,
When the wind blows,
The cradle will rock.
When the bough breaks,
The cradle will fall,
And down will come baby,
Cradle and all.

Star light, star bright

Star light, star bright,
First star I see tonight.
I wish I may, I wish I might,
Have the wish
I wish tonight.

Niddledy, noddledy

Niddledy, noddledy,
To and fro.
Tired and sleepy,
To bed we go.

Jump into bed,
Switch off the light,
Head on the pillow,
Shut your eyes tight.

Come, let's to bed

"Come, let's to bed,"
Says Sleepy Head.
"Wait a while,"
Says Slow.
"Put on the pan,"
Says Greedy Nan,
"We'll eat before we go."

13

14

Where should a baby rest?

Where should a baby rest?
Where but in its mother's arms?
Where can a baby lie
Half so safe from every harm?
Lulla, lulla, lullaby,
Softly sleep, my baby.
Lulla, lulla, lullaby,
Soft, soft, soft, my baby.

How many miles to Babyland?

How many miles to Babyland?
Anyone can tell.
Up one flight,
To your right,
Please to ring the bell.

The evening is coming

The evening is coming,
The sun sinks to rest,
The birds are all flying
Straight home to the nest.
"Caw," says the crow
As he flies overhead,
"It's time little children
Were going to bed!"

Now the day is over

Now the day is over,
Night is drawing nigh.
Shadows of the evening
Steal across the sky.

Moon, sun, shiny and silver

Moon, sun, shiny and silver,
Moon, sun, shiny and gold.
Moon, sun, shine on the young ones,
Shine until they grow old.

Shine, shine, shine, shine,
Shine until they grow old.

18

I see the moon

I see the moon,
And the moon sees me.
God bless the moon,
And God bless me.

The Sandman comes

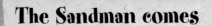

The Sandman comes,
The Sandman comes.
He has such pretty
Snow-white sand,
And well he's known
Throughout the land.
The Sandman comes.

Good night, sleep tight

Good night,
Sleep tight,
Wake up bright
In the morning light,
To do what's right
With all your might.

Come to the window

Come to the window, my baby, with me,
And look at the stars that shine on the sea.
There are two little stars that play at bo-peep,
With two little fishes far down in the deep,
And two little frogs cry, "Neap, neap, neap,
I see a dear baby that should be asleep!"

Baby's boat's
a silver moon

Baby's boat's a silver moon
Sailing in the sky,
Sailing over a sea of sleep
While the stars float by.

Sail, baby, sail,
Out upon the sea.
Only don't forget to sail
Back again to me.

Sleepy-time has come for my baby

Sleepy-time has come for my baby,
Baby now is going to sleep.
Kiss mummy goodnight
And we'll turn out the light,
While I tuck you in bed
'Neath your covers tight.
Sleepy-time has come for my baby,
Baby now is going to sleep.

Lullaby and goodnight

Lullaby and goodnight,
Mummy's delight,
Bright angels around
My darling shall stand.
They will guard you from harms,
You shall wake in my arms.
They will guard you from harms,
You shall wake in my arms.

Rock-a-bye, baby

Rock-a-bye, baby,
Your cradle is green,
Father's a nobleman,
Mother's a queen.
Betty's a lady and wears a gold ring,
And Johnny's a drummer,
And drums for the King.

Go to bed first

Go to bed first, a golden purse,
Go to bed second, a golden pheasant,
Go to bed third, a golden bird.

Sleep, little child

Sleep, little child, go to sleep,
Mummy is here by your bed.
Sleep, little child, go to sleep,
Rest on the pillow your head.

The world is silent and still,
The moon shines bright on the hill,
Then creeps past the windowsill.

Sleep, little child, go to sleep.
Oh sleep, go to sleep.

Go to bed late

Go to bed late,
Stay very small.
Go to bed early,
Grow very tall.

29

Notes on nursery rhymes

by Geraldine Taylor (Reading Consultant)

Nursery rhymes are such an important part of childhood, and make a vital contribution to early learning. Collections of nursery rhymes are among the first books we share with babies and children.

Rhyme and word-play stimulate language development and help children to recognise sounds. Feeling and beating rhythm, and joining in counting rhymes encourage early number ideas.

Babies will love to hear you say and sing these rhymes over and over again, and will respond to being gently rocked and jiggled.

Toddlers will love to take part in the actions themselves – with lots of clapping, miming and laughing.

The stories and characters of nursery rhymes will fascinate young children. Encourage them to think imaginatively by talking and wondering together about the people and animals. Nursery rhymes are a wonderful source of ideas for dressing-up and story telling.